# JUST MESSAGES
## "Changing the way of thinking"

# JUST MESSAGES
## "Changing the way of thinking"

## Contact links with Valerie E. Fontánez Santiago

Facebook
http://www.facebook.com/ValerieFontánezSantiago
http://www.facebook.com/ValerieFontánez
http:www.facebook.com/puntoalasunto
http://www.facebook.com/mvnmusic

Twitter
http;//twitter.com/valeriefontánez

Instagram
Valerie Fontánez Santiago

Email
valeriefontanez@gmail.com
Invencible0722@gmail.com

Whatsapp

Postal mail
P.O. Box 782316
Orlando, Florida 32878
P.O. Box 50001
Levittown, P.R. 00950

# JUST MESSAGES
## "Changing the way of thinking"

## INTRODUCTION

Through this little book I would like to bring you messages that inspire you, motivate you and help you see life from another point of view.

Help you modify your way of being and thinking about the situations that arise in our daily lives, we know that it is not easy, but it is our life and we have the obligation to live it to the fullest, always doing and thinking about things which are correct.

Through each message, perhaps you will remember some event in your life, and I only hope that with each of these words you learn to channel your actions and your emotions.

*"Silence has more than a thousand words, making it the most powerful weapon that human beings have in any situation."*

*Valerie E. Fontánez*

# JUST MESSAGES
## "Changing the way of thinking"

# JUST MESSAGES
## "Changing the way of thinking"

♥ Rights like titles are earned, not imposed.

♥ Pain has no tears, no words.

♥ Your thoughts will always be tied to your expressions.

♥ A strong woman knows how to keep her life in order, even with tears in her eyes she still stands.

♥ Someday I will see you, but I will not remember you.

♥ Perfect relationships don't exist, there are only lasting relationships for the rest of our lives.

♥ Betrayal doesn't destroy you, it builds you into a much stronger human being.

♥ I stopped being your mother, but you will never stop being my daughter.

♥ You can run from your past, but you can never hide from it.

♥ The past only affects those who remember it.

♥ I lived for you and you lived for yourself.

♥ Laugh for not crying.

♥ Children are Blessings, never curses.

# JUST MESSAGES
## "Changing the way of thinking"

♥ Forgiveness and forgetfulness, keys to follow.

♥ Not cold, not hot.

♥ Having Faith is walking towards success.

♥ Don't tell me I love you, with the same look you told me you wouldn't hurt me.

♥ Love when it is not true is like a tornado, when it arrives it lasts a short time, but it touches you, it shakes you, and when it leaves it destroys you.

♥ Just like you ever, because I will always be better than you.

♥ Courage is present when fear comes into your life.

♥ Fear stops being called fear, when you decide to be brave and fight.

♥ Before an attack, a defense.

♥ The essence of the human being is born from his thoughts and actions.

♥ We don't share the blood, but we share the heart.

♥ We know each other little and we love each other very much.

♥ Affection is imposed, love is earned.

# JUST MESSAGES
## "Changing the way of thinking"

♥ You already insulted my feelings, but you will never make me doubt my intelligence.

♥ Trust, believe and you will see the results.

♥ The right is earned.

♥ Rights are not imposed.

♥ Not having the right does not exempt you from responsibility.

♥ What doesn't work in your life, is because it doesn't belong to your life.

♥Always on my mind and fully in my heart.

♥ The woman who is happy will always shine with her own light.

♥ There is no better refuge than the heart of God, no safer place than his hands.

♥When you believe in God the impossible becomes possible.

♥ To be free it is not enough to believe it, you have to feel it.

♥A kiss and a hug when it is received with love and respect, will always be reciprocated in the same way.

# JUST MESSAGES
## "Changing the way of thinking"

♥ Remembering you is not calling you, it is not writing to you, it is not seeing you, it is not being by your side, remembering you is looking up to heaven and asking God to never leave you alone.

♥ A woman can be your princess, your queen, never your toy.

♥Happiness is within you.

♥ Pain has no tears, no words.

♥ When you're tired of dealing with so many people who are sick with evil, remember that you are too strong to let yourself be defeated.

♥ When human beings give you a thousand and one reasons not to continue, remember that God will give you a million opportunities to succeed.

♥ Today is now, tomorrow does not exist.

♥ Patience also has limits.

♥To listen you just have to hear.

♥ Although it is difficult to forgive, it is not impossible, to forgive is not to forget, it is just to turn the page, start over and be happy.

♥ Any idiot can have a child, but only a real MAN deserves to be called Dad.

# JUST MESSAGES
## "Changing the way of thinking"

♥ Excuses are given, when you don't have answers.

♥ True love is not shown with words, it is shown with deeds.

♥ It's not about changing your way of being, it's about changing your way of thinking.

♥ You never miss what your mind has already forgotten.

♥ Yesterday is over, tomorrow does not exist, and the future is unknown.

♥ Many times life puts us on paths where we don't know how to walk.

♥ The word Love means, Everything and Nothing, everything that makes you happy and nothing that makes you suffer.

♥On warning there is no deceit, "what is still is left still".

♥ Thoughts that only know how to dance in your head.

♥Your thoughts will always be tied to your expressions.

♥ Look within yourself for the solution to all your problems, even those that you create more exterior and material.

♥ The essence of the human being is born from his thoughts and actions, but not from his heart.

# JUST MESSAGES
## "Changing the way of thinking"

♥ I'd rather be hurt by a truth, than live in the shadows for a lie.

♥ You can't make others happy if you're not happy first.
♥When you love deeply, there is no need to post it.

♥ Offering friendship to those who ask for love is like giving bread to those who die of thirst.

♥When betrayal comes from who you least expect, you become a much stronger human being, and you learn never to trust.

♥ Disappointments that always come, from whom you least expect it.

♥ To be a good mother, you have to start by being a good woman.

♥Friendship can become love, but love can never become friendship.

♥When love ends, disappointment comes.

♥ To understand I have to understand and to understand I have to want.

♥ Giving in is not accepting.

♥ Not accepting reality is a way to evade your responsibility.

# JUST MESSAGES
## "Changing the way of thinking"

❤Long nights, endless days.

❤Trust is the basis of communication and understanding.

❤ To love you don't need to talk, or see people, just wake up and carry them in your heart.

❤ Love is born from the heart and not from the ego.

❤ To be happy you just have to be, period.

❤ The family that does not carry your blood is one that is chosen with the heart.

❤ The lie hurts, but the truth hurts.

❤ Go, go and don't look back, what is left is never recovered.

❤ Distance does not forget what the heart remembers.

❤ To love you have to forgive, to forgive you have to forget, today I tell you and tomorrow life will tell you.

❤ Patience with doubt is equal to betrayal.

❤ Doubt kills a real feeling.

❤ If you trust without a doubt everything will work out.

❤When there are doubts, trust is not complete.

# JUST MESSAGES
## "Changing the way of thinking"

❤ Dignity if you don't have it, no one will respect you.

❤ Money solves, but it doesn't always give you happiness.

❤ Believing for believing is equal to living without trusting.

❤ Memories are not saved, they are thrown away.

❤ Love is like the waves of the sea sometimes they are high and others they don't even feel.

❤Our destiny is within us; you just have to know how to decipher it.

❤ A blow hurts, you get over it and forget it, but words hurt more, they mark you forever and you never forget them.

❤Silence is the simplest way to express feelings.

❤ The illusion of seeing you again is the blessing of having you close.

❤ What doesn't destroy you is because it makes you much stronger.

❤ Loving the wrong person is often like Russian roulette, which often kills you.

❤ There is no disease that God does not heal for you.

# JUST MESSAGES
## "Changing the way of thinking"

♥ You lie to deceive and you do not realize that the deceived one is you.

♥ May your days always shine like sunlight.

♥ Thinking and Believing is not the same.

♥ Hiding a truth is not lying.

♥To be happy you don't have to use drugs, happiness lives within you.

♥ Orders are fulfilled and not discussed.

♥No one fools anyone, you only fool yourself.

♥ Mistakes that are not corrected become the worst horrors of your life.

♥ Courage = sadness
♥Sadness=disappointment
♥Disappointment=disappointment
♥ Disappointment = revenge.

♥ Loneliness seeks loneliness.

♥ Unconditional love is the one that lasts for a lifetime.

♥ The shine that a pregnant woman radiates is not overshadowed by anyone.

# JUST MESSAGES
## "Changing the way of thinking"

♥ Who sleeps with animals, wakes up full of shit.

♥ A last name does not make a human being.

♥Expecting the unexpected is like going to the sea and not knowing how to swim.

♥ Love is the mark that will prevail in you for a lifetime and even after death.

♥ The truth hurts, the lie destroys you.

♥ You can hurt me, but you will never get to hurt me.

♥ Betrayal just like money comes and goes, from where you least expect it.

♥ Children don't tie anyone.

♥ Negative thoughts will only attract courage, disappointment and anger.

♥If I understand, I understand you,

♥If I understand you, I accept you,

♥ And if I accept you, I forgive you.

♥ Pride and vanity are the curse of the human being.

♥ The complement for wisdom is reading.

♥ If they didn't teach you to be a good son, you can never be a good father.

♥ Love you maybe, hate you I don't know, forget you can be, never come back with you.

♥ If you attack me you hurt me and if you hurt me you offend me and if you offend me you don't love me.

# JUST MESSAGES
## "Changing the way of thinking"

♥ Confidence begins where insecurity ends.

♥ You can play with my mind, but never with my heart.

♥ Justifying mistakes with excuses is called cowardice.

♥ Life is too short to suffer for things that don't matter.

♥There are no problems that have no solution.

♥ I was, I am and forever I will be.

♥ I set you free to fly high.

♥ Human beings who are not honest are like cats, which are mostly treacherous.

♥ Infidelity will always be the fault of the most cowardly.

♥ When a relationship ends, regrets come.

♥Surrounded by many people, but completely alone.

♥ Just like you never, better than you always.

♥When you love-forgive,

♥If you forgive-trust

♥If you trust- they betray you,

♥ "Things of life."

♥ Don't talk about the past, unless it threatens your future.

♥ The past only affects those who remember it.

♥ Don't buy out of impulse, buy out of necessity.

# JUST MESSAGES
## "Changing the way of thinking"

♥ Don't swear with your head what you can't fulfill with your heart.

♥Life is like a period and a comma.

♥ Bad children are not always the product of a dysfunctional family.

♥ Perfect parents don't exist.

♥ Parents are not forever.

♥You can run from your past, but never hide from it, the past will always be part of your present.

♥ Of the brave brutes, the worst stories in life are written.

♥ The eyes express what your heart feels.

♥Marriage=divorce,
♥ Divorce = pension.

♥ Help yourself that I will help you or lose yourself that I will let you go.

♥ Forgiveness and forgetfulness, key to be able to continue.

♥ Only those who have no morals are offended.

♥ The more difficult your path is, the more your forces will multiply, the stronger your trials, the greater your

♥ When you claim something true and they don't answer you, it's because there is no answer to the truth.

♥ Strong women are those who make mistakes, admit them and learn from them, but most importantly, they know how to use them in their favor.

♥Strong women always face obstacles in their daily lives, sometimes with tears in their eyes, but they never lower their heads.

♥ Children are blessings, the moment your child becomes a business for you, at that moment you stop being a mother to become miserable.

♥ Human beings can control our thoughts, feelings and even our words, but we can never control what others can think, feel or say about us.

♥For everything in life there will always be a solution, look for it and you will find it.

♥ Bankruptcy, a way to evade responsibilities and usually only losers take advantage of it.

♥ You will always be the owner of your silences, but remember that you will also be the slave of your words.

# JUST MESSAGES
## "Changing the way of thinking"

♥Happiness and peace is not found through family, friends, children, it is not even found through your partner, true happiness is within you, within you, where not everyone knows how to arrive.

♥ Thoughts through your feelings.

♥ Never hide a secret for fear of losing something or someone, whoever wants to be with you will be there, they will accept you, they will understand you and they will stay.

♥In our walk through life we will find straight paths and others not so straight, only you will be the only one responsible for deciding where you want to walk.

♥ Life is not complicated, we ourselves are the ones who make it complicated with our actions.

♥ Never ask more than what they want to tell you, remember that the answers can cause you pain.

♥When you start thinking about solutions, that's when you really start to see the change.

♥ Don't be confused, love won't always be like foam, foam won't always be up.

♥ True feelings are expressed with facts and not with words.

♥ The essence of the human being is born from his thoughts and emotions, but not from his heart.

# JUST MESSAGES
## "Changing the way of thinking"

❤ I love you is a very strong word, don't say it if you don't really mean it.

❤They say that there is no better word than the one that is not said, and I say that there is no better answer than the one that is not given.

❤ A truly rich man is one whose children run into his arms, even when they have empty arms.

❤Living in the shadows is equal to not having life.

❤ Love with your mind and think with your heart.

❤To be the option of an election, better to be the truth than a lie.

❤People who are strong always continue standing and walking even in pain.

❤True love is only born from a true feeling.

❤ Pointless discussions only wear out your mind and wither your heart.

❤ It is human to be wrong and wise to rectify.

❤ Don't manage your life for others, manage it for yourself.

❤Arguments are a wrong way to express your feelings.

# JUST MESSAGES
## "Changing the way of thinking"

♥ Words have memory, listening to them you remember your past.

♥ Who makes you cry doesn't deserve your tears.

♥ Who wants to be with you runs and catches up with you.

♥ Pain is inevitable, but suffering is optional.

♥ Don't talk about people, talk to them in front of people.

♥ Neither happy nor angry make decisions.

♥ Wisdom, ability to apply what has been learned.

♥In confidence and tranquility is strength.

♥ Intelligence, ability to learn.

♥ Wisdom is not knowing, it is knowing what to do.

♥Your destiny will be only your responsibility.

♥ Live to be happy or suffer to remain paralyzed all your life.

♥ Being a victim is only your decision.

**JUST MESSAGES**
"Changing the way of thinking"


**THANKS**

To God, because without HIM nothing and with Him everything.

To my children, Mirta, Valerie, Nilka and Alejandro.

To my granddaughters, Sabrina and Daniela.

To Edgardo, for your support and unconditional love.

To more than a friend, to my sister Lourdes Santa, for never leaving me alone.

To my readers, thank you for your support in each of my books.

To Yoleiza Acosta, for your patience and for your help in each of my books.

To Professor Pedro Guevara, thank you for each of your translations, it is an honor for me to be able to count on you.

JUST MESSAGES
"Changing the way of thinking"


**Contact links with Valerie E. Fontánez Santiago**


Facebook
http://www.facebook.com/ValerieFontánezSantiago
http://www.facebook.com/ValerieFontánez
http:www.facebook.com/puntoalasunto
http://www.facebook.com/mvnmusic


Twitter
http;//twitter.com/valeriefontánez


Instagram
Valerie Fontánez Santiago


Email
valeriefontanez@gmail.com
Invencible0722@gmail.com


Whatsapp

Postal mail
P.O. Box 782316
Orlando, Florida 32878
P.O. Box 50001
Levittown, P.R. 00950

JUST MESSAGES
"Changing the way of thinking"

**Contact information for Yoleiza Acosta, Freelancer collaborating in the correction of my books.**

Facebook
https://www.facebook.com/yoleiza.acosta

Twitter
http://twitter.com/yoleizaacosta

Instagram
Yoleiza Acosta

Email
Yoleiza777@gmail.com
yoleizaacosta@gmail.com

Whatsapp
+5804168466703

**Comments:**

On this occasion I found several phrases that touched my heart, I think that all who read this book will feel identified with several of these wise words. Excellent material to meditate and delve into the realities of life. Excellent Valerie!!

JUST MESSAGES
"Changing the way of thinking"

## Contact information for Pedro Guevara, Translator of my books.

Facebook
https://www.facebook.com/pedroguevararojas

Twitter
http://twitter.com/pedroguevararojas

Email
pedroguevara1960@gmail.com

**Comments:**

Wise words that show the greatness of a brave heart, with each book I learn more, one of the most rewarding jobs I have had throughout my career, are without a doubt, the writings of Mrs. Valerie Fontánez. Blessings.

# JUST MESSAGES
## "Changing the way of thinking"

# JUST MESSAGES
## "Changing the way of thinking"

February 11, 2023. Copyright

www.ingramcontent.com/pod-product-compliance
Lightning Source LLC
Chambersburg PA
CBHW070646250726
48653CB00033B/1011